IT'S THE END OF THE WORLD!
SUPERVOLCANO ERUPTION

BY ALLAN MOREY

BELLWETHER MEDIA • MINNEAPOLIS, MN

Are you ready to take it to the extreme? Torque books thrust you into the action-packed world of sports, vehicles, mystery, and adventure. These books may include dirt, smoke, fire, and chilling tales.
WARNING: read at your own risk.

This edition first published in 2020 by Bellwether Media, Inc.

No part of this publication may be reproduced in whole or in part without written permission of the publisher.
For information regarding permission, write to Bellwether Media, Inc., Attention: Permissions Department,
6012 Blue Circle Drive, Minnetonka, MN 55343.

Library of Congress Cataloging-in-Publication Data

Names: Morey, Allan, author.
Title: Supervolcano Eruption / by Allan Morey.
Description: Minneapolis, MN : Bellwether Media, Inc., [2020] |
   Series: Torque: It's the End of the World! | Audience: Ages 7-12. |
   Audience: Grades 3 to 7.
Identifiers: LCCN 2019000942 (print) | LCCN 2019005222 (ebook) |
   ISBN 9781618916563 (ebook) | ISBN 9781644870853
   (hardcover : alk. paper)
Subjects: LCSH: Supervolcanoes–Juvenile literature. | Volcanism–Juvenile
   literature. | Natural disasters–Juvenile literature.
Classification: LCC QE521.3 (ebook) | LCC QE521.3 .M6445 2020 (print) |
   DDC 551.21–dc23
LC record available at https://lccn.loc.gov/2019000942

Text copyright © 2020 by Bellwether Media, Inc. TORQUE and associated logos are trademarks and/or registered trademarks of Bellwether Media, Inc. SCHOLASTIC, CHILDREN'S PRESS, and associated logos are trademarks and/or registered trademarks of Scholastic Inc., 557 Broadway, New York, NY 10012.

Editor: Rebecca Sabelko   Designer: Andrea Schneider

Printed in the United States of America, North Mankato, MN.

TABLE OF CONTENTS

BOOM!	4
THE ERUPTION BEGINS!	8
FORMING THE GREATEST VOLCANOES	14
HOW LIKELY IS A SUPERVOLCANO ERUPTION?	18
GLOSSARY	22
TO LEARN MORE	23
INDEX	24

BOOM!

The ground rumbles beneath you. You are knocked off your feet.

The ground continues to shake. You fear it is an earthquake. But then a volcanic **vent** erupts. **Fiery** hot ash shoots into the sky. You get to your feet and run.

The ground keeps shaking. Another vent bursts from the ground. You hear more rumbling. Then a third vent erupts.

DEADLY CLOUDS

Clouds of ash and toxic gases shoot out of volcanoes. They can reach speeds greater than 50 miles (80 kilometers) per hour. Their temperatures can reach more than 1,000 degrees Fahrenheit (538 degrees Celsius)!

ASH CLOUD

Seconds later, there is a massive explosion. You are thrown to the ground. A cloud of ash rushes outward. Everything in its path is **incinerated**.

THE ERUPTION BEGINS!

A supervolcano produces a **gigantic** volcanic eruption. Everything near its powerful blast is destroyed. It also shoots out ash, gases, and rocks. They spread out for hundreds of miles in every direction.

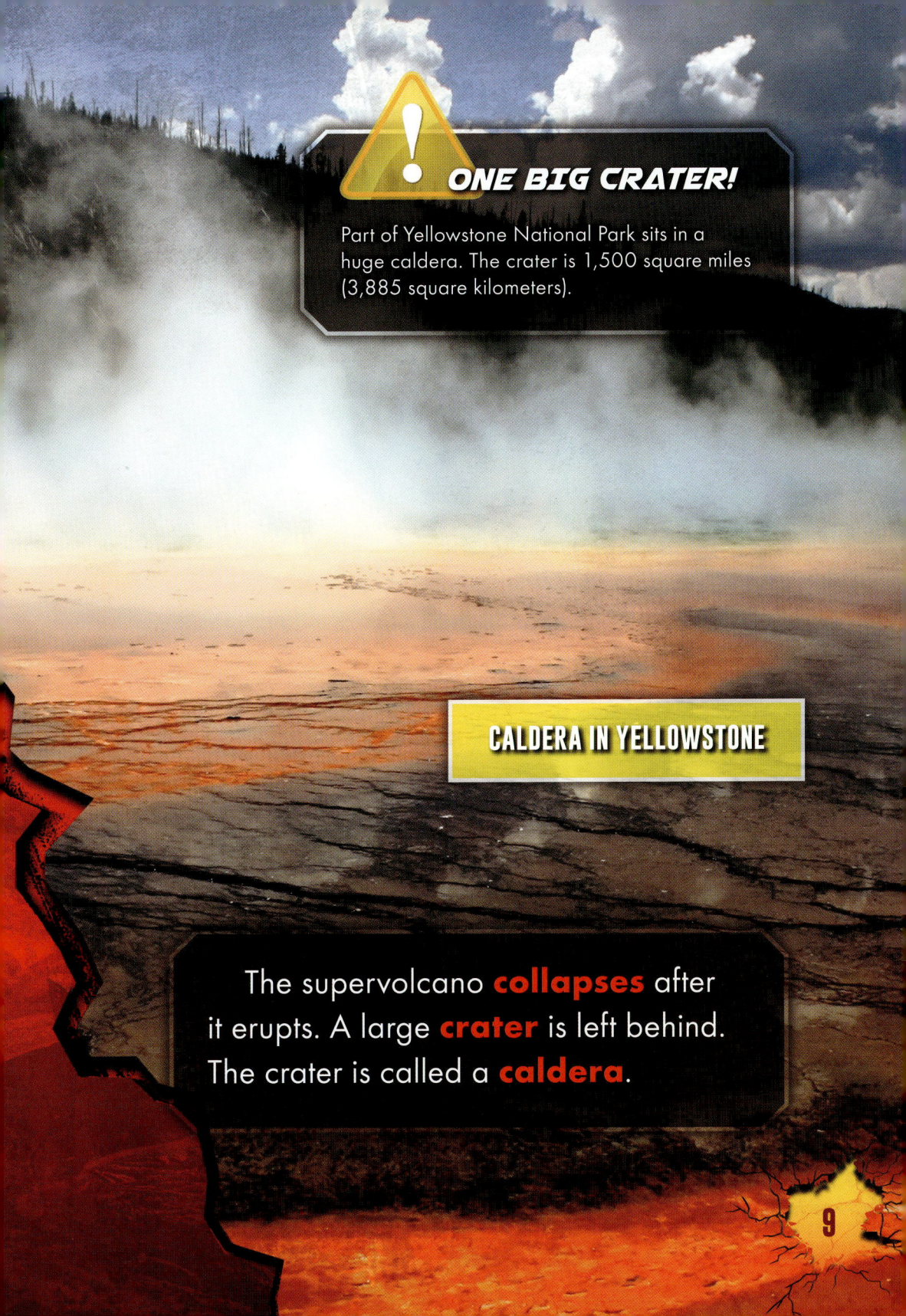

⚠ ONE BIG CRATER!

Part of Yellowstone National Park sits in a huge caldera. The crater is 1,500 square miles (3,885 square kilometers).

CALDERA IN YELLOWSTONE

The supervolcano **collapses** after it erupts. A large **crater** is left behind. The crater is called a **caldera**.

FIELDS OF ASH

The Campi Flegrei volcano is in Italy. It erupted about 39,000 years ago. Almost 8 inches (20 centimeters) of ash covered parts of Europe!

CRATER INSIDE CAMPI FLEGREI CALDERA

VOLCANIC ASH

Near the blast, everything is buried in ash. The ash that shoots into the sky is carried by the wind. The ground is covered in inches of ash for thousands of miles. Plants and animals die. People struggle to breathe.

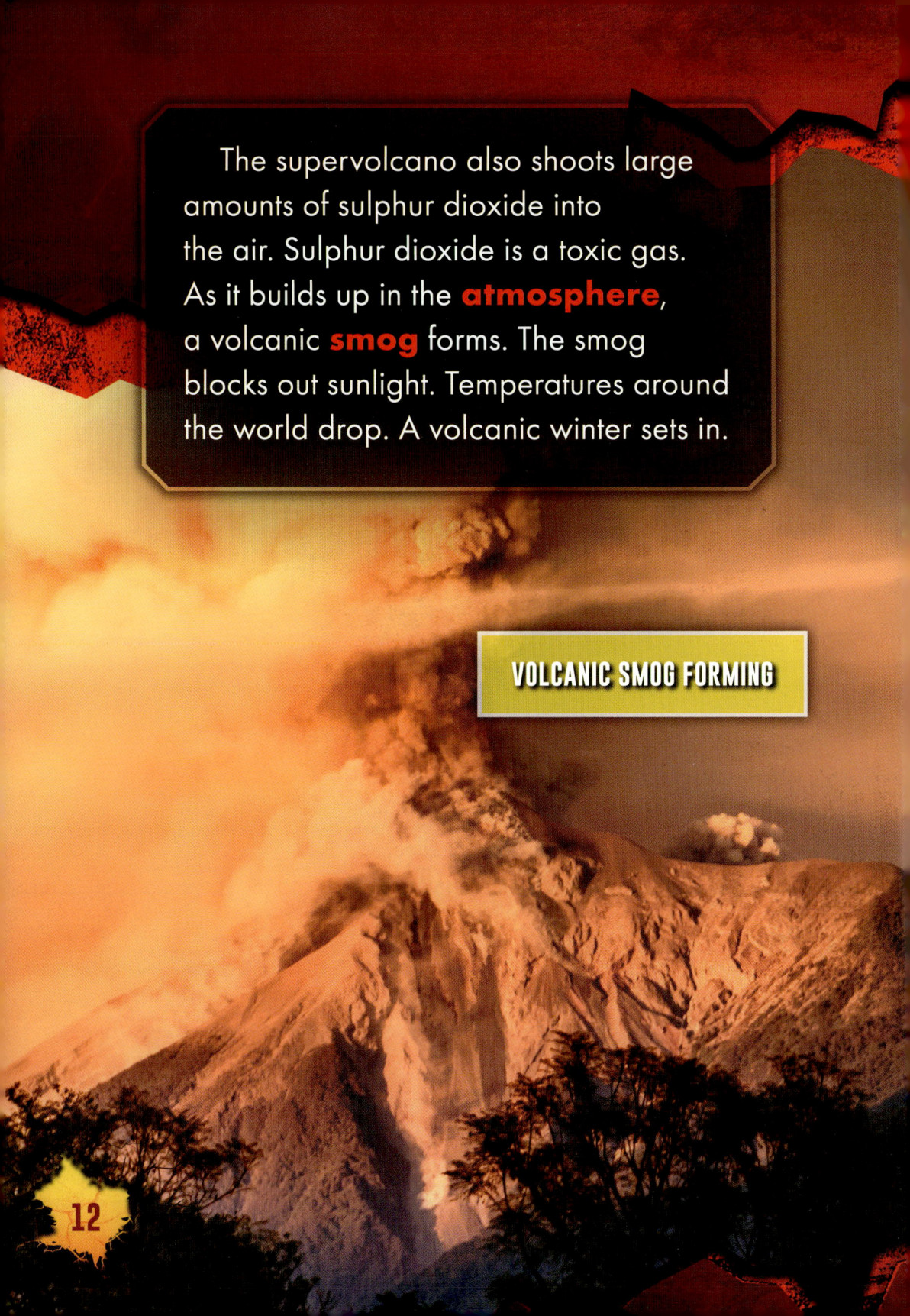

The supervolcano also shoots large amounts of sulphur dioxide into the air. Sulphur dioxide is a toxic gas. As it builds up in the **atmosphere**, a volcanic **smog** forms. The smog blocks out sunlight. Temperatures around the world drop. A volcanic winter sets in.

VOLCANIC SMOG FORMING

CHAIN REACTION

vents open until the blast turns into one huge explosion

lava races outward from the blast

a plume of ash shoots skyward

wind spreads the ash

plants and animals struggle to survive

ash and gas block out the sun and a volcanic winter begins

Forming the Greatest Volcanoes

Supervolcanoes are created as **magma** rises from Earth's **mantle**. The magma pools in Earth's **crust**. As the pool grows, it creates **pressure** beneath Earth's surface.

An eruption happens when the crust is no longer able to hold the pressure. Lava, ash, and gases shoot out.

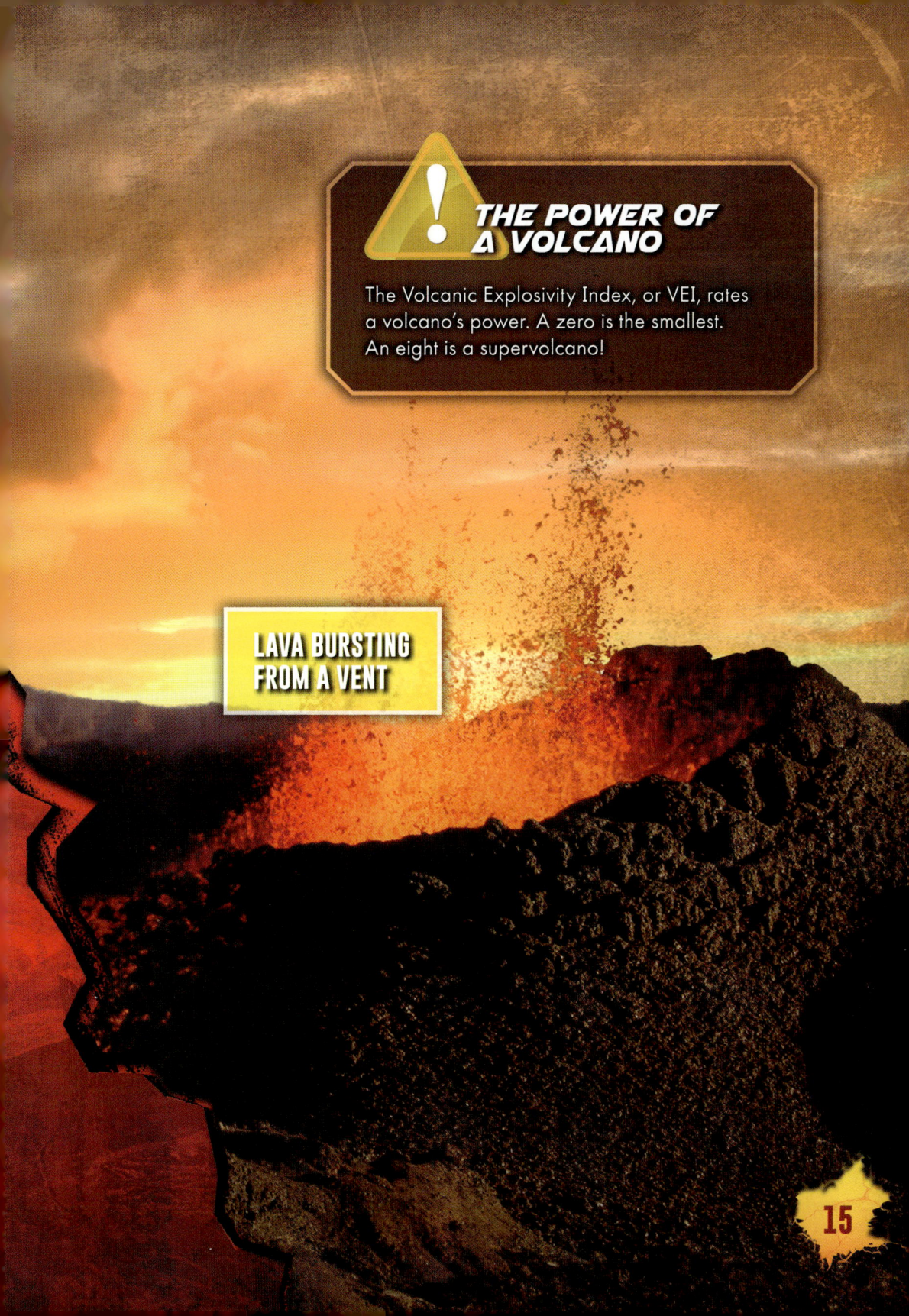

THE POWER OF A VOLCANO

The Volcanic Explosivity Index, or VEI, rates a volcano's power. A zero is the smallest. An eight is a supervolcano!

LAVA BURSTING FROM A VENT

After an eruption, a supervolcano collapses into its magma **chamber**. This creates a caldera.

GEYSER IN YELLOWSTONE

A LOOK BACK: MOUNT TAMBORO ERUPTION

1815

INDONESIA

The Mount Tamboro eruption blasted 60,000,000 tons of ash and rock into the air. The ash and rock blocked the sun and caused temperatures to drop about 5 degrees Fahrenheit (3 degrees Celsius).

Calderas form over hot spots in Earth's crust. In some calderas, the heat causes **geothermal** features. This includes hot springs and **geysers**. Other calderas fill up with water. They form large lakes.

HOW LIKELY IS A SUPERVOLCANO ERUPTION?

Supervolcanos have erupted in the past. The last eruption was about 27,000 years ago. Its caldera now forms Lake Taupo in New Zealand.

The Phlegraean Fields is in Italy. It is one of the most active volcanic areas in the world. But a major eruption is not likely to happen there for thousands of years.

LAKE TOBA

The Toba supervolcano in Indonesia erupted about 70,000 years ago. Its caldera now forms Lake Toba.

LAKE TAUPO

Yellowstone is one of the best known supervolcanoes. Its last supereruption was more than 600,000 years ago!

YELLOWSTONE HOT SPRING

YELLOWSTONE HOT SPRING

The magma below Yellowstone has created hot springs and bubbling mud pots. But the only thing to erupt there recently are geysers. Scientists do not believe a supervolcano is likely to happen any time soon. We are safe for now!

GLOSSARY

atmosphere—the gases that surround Earth

caldera—a giant crater created by a supervolcano eruption

chamber—an enclosed space

collapses—caves or falls in

crater—a deep hole in the surface of the earth

crust—Earth's outer layer

fiery—having or making fire

geothermal—having to do with heat from inside the earth

geysers—holes in the ground that shoot out hot water and steam

gigantic—huge

incinerated—burned to ashes

magma—hot liquid rock below the surface of the earth

mantle—the layer below Earth's crust

pressure—a physical force pushing against an object

smog—fog mixed with smoke

vent—an opening in Earth's crust from which magma can erupt

TO LEARN MORE

AT THE LIBRARY

Hoena, Blake. *Can You Survive a Supervolcano Eruption?: An Interactive Doomsday Adventure.* North Mankato, Minn.: Capstone Press, 2016.

Maurer, Tracy Nelson. *The World's Worst Volcanic Eruptions.* North Mankato, Minn.: Capstone Press, 2019.

Nagle, Frances. *Yellowstone National Park.* New York, N.Y.: Gareth Stevens Publishing, 2016.

ON THE WEB

FACTSURFER

Factsurfer.com gives you a safe, fun way to find more information.
1. Go to www.factsurfer.com
2. Enter "supervolcano eruption" into the search box and click 🔍.
3. Select your book cover to see a list of related web sites.

INDEX

ash, 4, 6, 7, 8, 10, 11, 14
atmosphere, 12
blast, 8, 11
caldera, 9, 10, 16, 17, 18, 19
Campi Flegrei, Italy, 10
chain reaction, 13
crater, 9, 10
crust, 14, 17
earthquake, 4
gases, 6, 8, 12, 14
geothermal features, 17
geysers, 16, 17, 21
hot springs, 17, 20, 21
Lake Taupo, New Zealand, 18, 19
Lake Toba, Indonesia, 19

lava, 14, 15
magma, 14, 21
magma chamber, 16
mantle, 14
Mount Tamboro eruption, 17
mud pots, 21
Phlegraean Fields, Italy, 18
pressure, 14
rocks, 8
scientists, 21
smog, 12
sulphur dioxide, 12
vent, 4, 5, 6, 15
Volcanic Explosivity Index, 15
volcanic winter, 12
Yellowstone, 9, 16, 20, 21

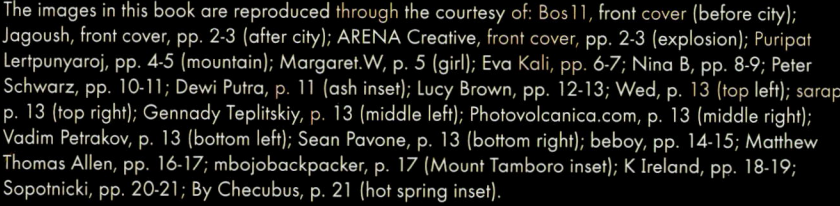

The images in this book are reproduced through the courtesy of: Bos11, front cover (before city); Jagoush, front cover, pp. 2-3 (after city); ARENA Creative, front cover, pp. 2-3 (explosion); Puripat Lertpunyaroj, pp. 4-5 (mountain); Margaret.W, p. 5 (girl); Eva Kali, pp. 6-7; Nina B, pp. 8-9; Peter Schwarz, pp. 10-11; Dewi Putra, p. 11 (ash inset); Lucy Brown, pp. 12-13; Wed, p. 13 (top left); sarap, p. 13 (top right); Gennady Teplitskiy, p. 13 (middle left); Photovolcanica.com, p. 13 (middle right); Vadim Petrakov, p. 13 (bottom left); Sean Pavone, p. 13 (bottom right); beboy, pp. 14-15; Matthew Thomas Allen, pp. 16-17; mbojobackpacker, p. 17 (Mount Tamboro inset); K Ireland, pp. 18-19; Sopotnicki, pp. 20-21; By Checubus, p. 21 (hot spring inset).